Narcissism

Break Free From The Grasp Of Manipulation And Personality Disorders

(Unveiling The Egotistical Nature Of A Self-centered Narcissistic Individual)

Clifford Odonnell

TABLE OF CONTENT

Introduction 1

Male And Female Narcissism 40

Exploitation Is Prevalent 70

Take Control Back 112

Are You Equipped To Effectively Handle An Individual With Narcissistic Tendencies? Tips And Strategies 150

Conclusion 165

Introduction

There is a rapidly spreading global silent pandemic. It exhibits a lesser degree of prominence and translucency compared to the majority. Based on the findings of experts in the field of psychology, secondhand smoke of mental health is a recognized phenomenon. The phenomenon that I am referring to is commonly known as narcissism. It is evident that narcissism is becoming increasingly prevalent in society. This issue presents a contemporary concern.

Societal phenomena such as social media, where the primary focus lies in comparing oneself to others, contribute to the increased prevalence of narcissistic tendencies. The shallowness of our current era, coupled with the prioritization of consumerism, intensifies the prominence of narcissistic inclinations, rendering emotions and empathy dispensable.

Narcissism can be classified into four primary categories, including grandiose, malignant, covert, and communal narcissism. Detecting the behavioural patterns linked to narcissism presents a formidable challenge.

Nevertheless, the objective of this literary work is to unveil these behaviors and cultivate an understanding of them, as one may unwittingly fall prey to them. As an individual who has suffered the effects of narcissism, the result can be profoundly destructive and deeply unsettling. You experience a constant sense of tiptoeing and uncertainty, unsure of when the situation may escalate or when outbursts of rage might be unleashed. You are experiencing self-doubt due to the emotional manipulation perpetrated by the narcissist.

Numerous individuals experience hardship as a result of their narcissistic partners, yet they remain unaware of the fact that they are entangled with a narcissistic individual. Now is the opportune moment to ascribe a label to the upheaval and perplexity encountered within your romantic alliance. As you acquire knowledge about narcissistic behavioral tendencies, you will come to realize their predictability and the fact that they occur in an alternating manner. Regrettably, narcissism is not unfamiliar, rather it manifests as covert and elusive due to our lack of expertise in its detection.

The preservation of one's mental well-being is a crucial aspect of our overall health, and the ramifications of being involved with a narcissistic partner can extend to the point of inflicting emotional and psychological harm. It is imperative for all of us to acquire knowledge on this subject, thereby underscoring its significance.

Welcome to this comprehensive discussion on the crucial aspects pertaining to narcissism, and the essential insights one should be aware of when navigating encounters with narcissistic individuals, particularly within the context of romantic relationships.

Vulnerable Narcissism Traits

The alternate form of narcissist, referred to as vulnerable, does not manifest overt narcissistic traits. In reality, they give the impression of being fragile, lacking in self-assurance, and exceedingly susceptible (traits that genuinely belong to them). They lack the allure and exuberance typically associated with an extravagant narcissistic individual. Indeed, they possess a lack of awareness regarding their own value, which subsequently leads them to prefer solitude. They make an effort to prevent finding themselves in circumstances where their weaknesses are poised to be revealed.

Emotionally aloof and highly susceptible to criticism.

A vulnerable narcissist exhibits a heightened level of emotional sensitivity to experiences of emotional harm. Indeed, individuals must exercise utmost caution when communicating with them. Nevertheless, they lack awareness of the emotions of others. They fail to comprehend the fact that their conduct has an impact on others and can have negative consequences. Vulnerable narcissists exhibit such profound preoccupation with their anxieties and feelings of shame that they are consequently oblivious to their surroundings. They like to be distant from people because they always fear judgment and humiliation of some kind.

Vulnerable narcissism exhibits elevated levels of neuroticism, resulting in a propensity for introversion, a tendency toward pessimism, and an increased susceptibility to depression. As vulnerable narcissists maintain a belief that they are subject to abandonment and rejection by others, they tend to engage in self-imposed isolation in an effort to gain acceptance from their peers. Additionally, they tend to isolate themselves socially as a means of evading interpersonal interactions. Vulnerable narcissists experience apprehension about potential exposure to ridicule and harassment due to their authentic selves when encountering others. They often exhibit pronounced emotional instability, resulting in episodes of anger and attribution of their emotions to external sources. They also struggle with placing their trust in individuals.

Vulnerable narcissists possess an innate sense of insecurity regarding receiving criticism, thereby rendering them challenging companions. As an example, individuals may aspire to garner admiration from their colleagues in a professional setting, simultaneously harboring apprehension regarding emotional harm. This is attributable to their inherent psychological vulnerability and the presence of unwarranted demands from others. Consequently, in the absence of receiving recognition or attention, which they seemingly do not actively seek, they experience an intensified feeling of shame.

Rife with suspicion and resentment

They experience a sense of anger due to the growing conviction that the world unjustly discriminates against them. They hold the belief that external individuals bear responsibility for any adverse incidents they have encountered. The impression they hold of themselves, characterized by negativity, is what precipitates inconsequential occurrences within the realms of their imagination. Vulnerable narcissists construct their own narrative, assume every role independently, and subsequently reveal the outcome to those in their vicinity, leaving everyone perplexed and filled with a sense of consternation.

A vulnerable narcissist experiences a combination of intense pride and profound shame, causing them to exhibit heightened sensitivity towards even the most subtle forms of criticism. Individuals with narcissistic tendencies often experience discomfort when they become the object of laughter, as it triggers their insecurities and challenges their self-image. Nevertheless, they readily engage in the act of mocking others without hesitation.

Whether they are their own relatives, acquaintances, or even individuals they encounter by chance, individuals universally experience stress when engaging with a vulnerable narcissist. Nevertheless, it appears that the narcissist remains oblivious to this reality or consciously opts to deny the need for rectifying their distorted conduct.

Hence, whether one displays grandiose or vulnerable narcissistic traits, individuals of both personality types pose challenges in various relationships, particularly intimate bonds like marriage and parenthood. They exhibit acts of benevolence and affection under the guise of ulterior motives, harboring resentment towards individuals whom they rely on.

Grandiose vs. Vulnerable Narcissism

Based on empirical evidence and scholarly inquiries, it has been observed that in the context of agreeableness, vulnerable narcissists tend to exhibit a significant association with trust, while demonstrating minimal inclination towards modesty. Conversely, individuals exhibiting grandiose narcissism demonstrate a significant association with modesty, while concurrently displaying a pronounced deficit in trust. Although vulnerable and grandiose personalities share antagonistic behavior traits, the underlying motivations driving these behavioral patterns may differ. A vulnerable narcissist, as an illustration, might exhibit heightened hostility in their demeanor, whereas a grandiose narcissist is inclined towards self-enhancement.

Self-worth in the Divergent Personality Profiles

Furthermore, individuals who exhibit grandiose and vulnerable narcissism demonstrate their affiliation with self-worth in distinct manners. A self-aggrandizing narcissist generally exhibits a slightly to moderately favorable association, whereas a susceptible narcissist displays a moderately adverse correlation with their self-worth. The distinct correlations between the two types of narcissistic individuals and self-esteem imply fundamental distinctions in the essence of these concepts or theories.

Perception of their respective marital partners

Additionally, individuals who possess any form of affiliation with either susceptible or grandiose narcissists also perceive them in a distinctive manner. Spouses of grandiose or vulnerable narcissists typically perceive them as domineering, merciless, uncompromising, hypocritical, contentious, arrogant, opportunistic, and exacting. Nonetheless, individuals wedded to grandiose narcissists perceived their partners as overt, perceptive, presumptuous, assertive, vocal, and unwavering.

Conversely, individuals married to vulnerable narcissists perceived their partners as exhibiting emotional volatility, anxiety, defensiveness, bitterness, and restlessness, often exhibiting tendencies to excessively ruminate and express grievances.

Prominent exhibitionists exhibit characteristics that resemble those of individuals with antisocial tendencies and potentially intense personality disorders. In contrast, susceptible narcissists appear to display traits reminiscent of detached and borderline personality disorders. Curiously, when accounting for their propensity towards negative emotions, vulnerable narcissists exhibit a higher likelihood of being diagnosed with borderline personality disorder as opposed to narcissistic personality disorder. Furthermore, these findings indicate that vulnerable narcissists, akin to individuals diagnosed with borderline personality disorder (BPD), exhibit no contemplation of self-harm or engagement in suicidal behavior.

Observing and Analyzing Social Behavior in Various Situations

In a social context, it is plausible to discern and differentiate the two classifications of narcissists based on their demeanor and conduct. An individual with an inflated sense of self-importance exhibits exceptional interpersonal abilities. Their ability to captivate and charm individuals within a group setting through their eloquent speech and engaging demeanor is rather remarkable. The situation differs when it comes to a vulnerable narcissist, as they exhibit inadequate interpersonal abilities. Their reserved and apprehensive nature in social settings could possibly limit their ability to draw a large crowd. One notable distinction between the two personality types lies in the fact that grandiose narcissists exhibit entrepreneurial qualities, along with a forthright and resolute disposition, as they actively pursue their objectives in their quest for elevated success. In contrast, vulnerable narcissists lack the same level of bravery and resolve. Indeed, they exhibit heightened self-protective tendencies and are solely focused on mitigating the extent of their failures.

Propensity Towards Social Standing and Integration

Based on multiple academic studies, researchers endeavored to evaluate the prevalence of the two primary manifestations of narcissism among a cohort of 676 individuals residing in the United States. Additionally, they conducted an evaluation of the fervor with which they aspired to attain a specific social standing and acceptance, while also assessing the extent to which they believed they had successfully attained their objectives.

The findings demonstrated that individuals classified as grandiose and vulnerable narcissists exhibited a strong and fervent desire for a specific social status. The sole discrepancy lay in the fact that grandiose narcissists believed they had accomplished the desired social status, whereas vulnerable narcissists perceived themselves as falling short of the social standing they believed they merited and were entitled to.

Moreover, grandiose narcissists did not truly achieve integration into society, nor did they exhibit much concern for it. In contrast, vulnerable narcissists displayed a strong desire for social acceptance, yet regrettably, failed to attaain it. Consequently, individuals exhibiting grandiose narcissism appeared to derive satisfaction from their perceived attainment of societal ambitions. Conversely, those displaying vulnerable narcissism did not share the same sentiment.

Individuals exhibiting both grandiose and vulnerable narcissistic traits are driven by a need to receive admiration and respect from those around them. However, it is solely the ostentatious type of narcissist who is capable of occupying the center of attention and reveling in their triumphs. The vulnerable type of narcissist often assumes a passive role, unsure of how to proceed, and relies on others to bestow unwarranted recognition upon them. They harbor a sense of resentment as they strive for recognition and admiration, yet their endeavors fall short due to their inherent timidness and pessimistic outlook.

MALE AND FEMALE NARCISSISM

Ongoing debates persist among social scientists concerning the divergences and parallels pertaining to narcissism between men and women. An idea that sparks controversy is the notion that certain narcissistic attributes, such as aggression, competitiveness, and aloofness, are deemed more socially acceptable when exhibited by men rather than women. Consequently, it is more probable for narcissistic women to conceal their inherent characteristics.

According to a study undertaken by psychological researchers, it has been observed that, over the course of time, men exhibit a greater propensity towards narcissism compared to women. Nevertheless, irrespective of gender, individuals harboring narcissistic traits exhibit an unwavering inclination to incessantly pursue attention and engage in manipulating others. In the aforementioned investigation, the researchers also discovered that women characterized as possessing a high degree of narcissism frequently opt for attire that is more revealing, while their male counterparts frequently engage in conceited and vacuous self-promotion. Additionally, individuals of both genders have a predilection towards engaging in short-term sexual relationships, as evidenced by their respective personal backgrounds.

An additional investigation demonstrated that male and female individuals exhibiting narcissistic traits consistently present themselves in a fashionably and impeccably attired manner, adorned in contemporary garments that distinguish them from others. However, conversational skills do not align with their aforementioned qualities, as narcissists frequently manifest disagreement with others and frequently resort to the utilization of sexual language in discourse.

In the realm of interpersonal connections with narcissistic individuals, it is notable that male narcissists possess distinct characteristics. Due to women typically gravitating towards enduring partnerships, they possess a heightened ability to identify narcissistic men.

However, given that the majority of males do not inherently oppose casual encounters, they remain relatively unaffected by the presence of self-absorbed women they encounter.

Narcissists and Attraction

Females who display emotional or nurturing characteristics are more inclined to be attracted to individuals exhibiting narcissistic behavior. The underlying explanation for this phenomenon could potentially lie in their perception of their own capacity to alter the narcissist, an endeavor that would, in all likelihood, prove futile. According to a study conducted in the

United States, it has been observed that women tend to display a tendency towards attraction to the assertive attributes exhibited by individuals with narcissistic qualities, especially during their fertile phase.

In regard to women with narcissistic tendencies, it is probable that they will seek out males who possess significant wealth, influence, or a combination of both. This is due to their desire to acquire access to a more luxurious lifestyle, which they accomplish by cunningly manipulating the partner who possesses the means to fulfill their desires. Upon deeper reflection, it becomes evident that locating an individual labeled as a "gold digger" lacking narcissistic attributes would prove to be a formidable task.

Certainly, it should be noted that this matter is not simply a matter of absolutes. Within this context, it is important to acknowledge the existence of narcissistic men who purposefully pursue affluent and influential women, as well as narcissistic women who exhibit a preference for men who deeply admire and are willing to provide for them.

These concepts have been derived from a range of psychological studies to illustrate that there exist significant dissimilarities in the characteristics of male and female narcissists, despite the potential for some ambiguity in certain instances. A prevailing similarity observed among male and female narcissists is their preference for individuals who affirm and validate their self-image. After the relationship becomes stagnant, they proceed to pursue the next potential avenue for validation of their ego.

They gaslight you

Gaslighting, an aspect intrinsic to narcissistic behavior, represents a manifestation of emotional maltreatment and manipulation. Specifically, when confronted with perceived threats to their authority or the possibility of abandonment, individuals with Narcissistic Personality Disorder (NPD) may engage in the deliberate dissemination of falsehoods, erroneously accuse others, manipulate the truth, and eventually manipulate your perception of reality.

The subsequent are manifestations of gas lighting:

• You no longer identify with the individual you used to be.

• In contrast to previous circumstances, your level of confidence has diminished while your level of apprehension has heightened.

• You often inquire if you are overly sensitive.

• You hold the belief that all your actions are erroneous.

• On each occasion that an issue arises, you consistently assume responsibility for it.

• You seem to be expressing apologies frequently. • You are employing the phrase 'I'm sorry' quite frequently. • It appears that you are using apologetic language extensively. • You are frequently offering apologies.

• You perceive an underlying unease, yet you find yourself unable to ascertain its precise nature.

•You often question the appropriateness of your reactions towards your partner.

• You employ reasoning to explain your partner's actions.

They employ this strategy to undermine the credibility of others, with the aim of asserting their own sense of superiority. Peykar claims that narcissists employ manipulative tactics with the intention of eliciting adoration from others, as they derive gratification from this behavior.

They consistently refrain from extending apologies as they firmly believe in their infallibility.

Frequently, one encounters discussions regarding the disdainful dispositions and conceited conduct exhibited by individuals diagnosed with Narcissistic Personality Disorder (NPD). As a result of this, confronting a narcissist may appear exceedingly challenging.

With a narcissist, there is no room for discussion or accommodation because they are invariably correct, according to Tawwab. They will not consistently identify a difference in opinion as such. They will interpret it solely as them conveying a perceived truth to you.

According to Peykar, when your companion elicits such emotions as:

• is not hearing you.

• won't comprehend you.

• displays a lack of willingness to assume responsibility for their contribution to a problem.

• does not make attempts to negotiate.

Weiler recommends refraining from engaging in negotiations and conflicts, while acknowledging that terminating the relationship remains the most advisable course of action when encountering individuals with NPD.

The lack of restraint and a direct conflict is what provokes a volatile response in individuals with narcissistic traits. She offers the advice that it is preferable to minimize the amount of control they have over you by refraining from engaging in resistance.

Additionally, they rarely extend apologies due to their steadfast conviction in their own infallibility.

They react violently when you let them know you're done.

Individuals with Narcissistic Personality Disorder often exhibit a propensity for reacting aggressively towards others when their self-esteem is undermined, rendering them highly susceptible to experiences of shame and humiliation.

Peykar asserts that expressing your desire to terminate the relationship explicitly would prompt them to deliberately harm you in response.

Their sense of self-importance is so gravely injured that it provokes a vehement and hostile response towards those they perceive as having mistreated them. Given that all others are at fault, this is the situation at hand. "In addition to the aforementioned division," she continues.

Chapter 3: Techniques of Narcissistic Manipulation.

Due to the prevalence of manipulation among narcissists, it is of utmost importance for you to acquire extensive knowledge regarding this deceitful behavior.

Initially, it is important to acknowledge that there exist various classifications of manipulative individuals, among which a narcissist has the capability to assume any desired classification. Indeed, the outcome will frequently be contingent upon the individual's desired objectives in the given scenario.

A form of manipulation that can occur is that of the intimidator. As previously indicated, individuals with narcissistic tendencies frequently employ threats as a potent means of manipulation. You might have frequently encountered instances where your mother conveyed the message that failure to comply with her desires would subject you to physical harm. It is possible that she conveyed to you that failing to comply with her wishes would result in the cessation of her affection towards you. A narcissistic mother resorts to employing an array of threats towards her child.

While occasional instances of parental disciplinary measures may involve threatening a child, it is crucial to recognize that a narcissistic individual tends to escalate and intensify such threats. For instance, a typical parent would refrain from conveying to their child that failing to fulfill their responsibilities would result in a withdrawal of parental affection. This threat solely originates from a parent who exhibits narcissistic tendencies. The majority of parents harbor an unwavering, unconditional love for their children and would never entertain the notion of expressing a lack of love towards them on account of their failure to comply with instructions. Indeed, the majority of parents anticipate occasional instances where their children will disobey or fail to promptly comply with their requests.

Nevertheless, a narcissistic parent harbors the belief that their child should unquestioningly adhere to their requests, as this is emblematic of a narcissist's mindset. A narcissistic individual holds the belief that her significance is of such magnitude that there exists no valid justification for noncompliance with her requests, particularly when she solicits assistance from her own daughter.

The second category of manipulation pertains to individuals who employ guilt tripping techniques. When employing such manipulation tactics, a narcissist seeks to instill feelings of guilt within you as a means of influencing your actions and beliefs. Regardless of the magnitude of your efforts to emancipate yourself from the burden of guilt, the narcissist possesses an inherent ability to manipulate your emotions in such a manner that instills within you an overwhelming sense of being the most morally depraved individual imaginable, devoid of any concern for their well-being. The individual possesses the ability to manipulate you into perceiving it as a reflection of your own lack of concern towards them, rather than acknowledging their own lack of care for you. Hence, in the perspective of a narcissist, what reason would she have to concern herself with you if you do not reciprocate the same level of care for her. To put it differently, the guilt tripper is frequently employed as a manipulative strategy by a narcissist with the intention of shifting blame onto you for a particular matter.

The third form of manipulation employed by a narcissist involves engaging in competition. Although many parents frequently resort to employing a playful element of rivalry among their children to motivate them to complete tasks, such as tidying up their rooms or racing to the car, a narcissist will elevate this dynamic to a more extreme level. Furthermore, it can be observed that a narcissistic individual is prone to incorporating additional strategies of manipulation into their competitive behavior, with the underlying purpose of attaining their desired outcomes from the targeted individual. For instance, she may assert that failing to secure a scholarship is indicative of insufficient devotion towards her. This is frequently a matter beyond your full jurisdiction. For instance, it is possible to exert maximum effort and still not attain the scholarship, as the committee's judgment determined that another candidate was more deserving of the award. Nevertheless, by virtue of your failure to emerge victorious, it can be inferred that your love for your mother was inadequate. To put it differently, if you happen to be unsuccessful in a competition, it could be inferred that your level of affection towards your mother may be insufficient, as it suggests insufficient effort on your part to honor her. This serves as an illustration of a situation wherein the intensity of competition is heightened, indicating the approach a narcissist may adopt when facing competition.

Conversely, it is possible that your mother frequently engaged in competition with you as a means of asserting her superiority. As an illustration, she may have proposed that you engage in a race, partake in a game, or engage in a competition in which she excels. Subsequently, following your defeat against her, she would adopt a condescending attitude by asserting that your lack of strength and intelligence rendered you incapable of achieving victory. Additionally, she may assert that it is implausible for you to triumph against her, as she consistently outperforms. Nevertheless, in the event that you were ever to emerge victorious, it is highly probable that you would incur her ire. As an instance, she may level allegations of infidelity against you, subsequently subjecting you to punitive measures. Furthermore, she may employ tactics of emotional manipulation, such as appealing to your sense of guilt, in order to elicit negative feelings regarding your triumph.

The narcissist engaging in self-esteem assault represents the fourth variation of manipulation. This represents a frequently observed tactic employed by individuals with narcissistic traits, as it serves as a means for them to elevate their self-worth above that of others, a behavior that is commonly observed. If she possesses the capacity to denigrate you for a specific matter, she is also capable of enhancing her own image through persuasive speech. A self-absorbed individual is aware of the necessity to diminish one's self-esteem in order to reduce their perceived level of threat.

The most significant issue associated with this form of manipulation is the lack of concern displayed by your mother regarding the extent of harm she inflicts upon you. This is frequently attributable to her aim of systematically undermining your emotional and psychological resilience, resulting in your perpetual doubt regarding the possibility of surpassing her achievements in any aspect, even when you objectively outperform her. Undoubtedly, the detrimental effects of low self-esteem extend far beyond commonly recognized implications.

The fifth form of manipulation manifests itself in the utilization of the practice known as silent treatment. Although it is probable that a child may occasionally resort to giving their parent the cold shoulder, particularly during their adolescent years, it is highly uncommon for a parent to employ the silent treatment tactic, unless they exhibit narcissistic tendencies and frequently rely on manipulative behavior to achieve their objectives. For instance, as adolescence dawns upon you, it is likely that you commenced challenging the narcissistic tendencies exhibited by your mother, akin to the common demeanor of teenagers who challenge their parental figures. Although you may have exercised greater prudence in the manner and content of your opposition to your mother, out of concern for provoking her anger, you nevertheless contested her. Indeed, when confronted with a challenge, a narcissist disapproves greatly and promptly resorts to employing manipulative tactics to fervently halt any furtherance of the said challenge. One potential method could be employing the tactic of non-response, particularly if one has previously yielded to this type of manipulative behavior.

When your mother employed the silent treatment, she would refrain from engaging in any kind of communication, regardless of the circumstances, be it when you sought her assistance or attempted to offer her something, she would adamantly refuse to acknowledge/respond. In fact, sometimes a parent will refuse to look at her child while she is using the silent treatment. Certainly, this is merely an additional strategic maneuver with the intention of achieving her objectives and inducing in you a sense of remorse for your actions. Similar to other methods of manipulation, this is a strategy employed by her to instill a sense of fear within you. It serves as an endeavor to acquaint you with her abilities, should you dare to question her once more.

Lacking Empathy

An evident characteristic of a mother displaying narcissistic tendencies is her pronounced absence of empathy, commonly referred to as the capacity to extend compassion towards an individual facing distressing circumstances. Nonetheless, empathy can be experienced through various emotional states. In truth, individuals who are perceived as having a high degree of empathy possess the ability to discern and internalize the emotions of others to such an extent that they begin to experience them personally. Irrespective of whether an individual experiences sadness, anger, or joy, a person with empathy will be capable of sensing and comprehending those emotions.

This gift is generally well-received. Individuals possessing proficient empathic abilities can frequently employ said skills to provide assistance to others. Nevertheless, in the absence of empathy, an individual will be unable to perceive or resonate with the emotional experiences of others. As a result, she will exhibit a lack of concern towards understanding the individual's emotional state. To some extent, if it has no impact on her, it holds no significance. This accurately depicts the emotional experience of an individual with narcissistic traits. She displays no concern for any emotions that do not belong to her. Regardless of whether her daughter is experiencing sadness due to a breakup or happiness due to achieving a high score on her final exam, these emotional states hold no significance for her self-absorbed mother.

If you possess inquiries about whether your mother experiences challenges in showcasing empathy, there exist a multitude of indicators that can aid in discerning this. Undoubtedly, one of the initial indications is her lack of concern for the emotions of others. Additional indicators include a propensity for swift criticism and hasty formation of judgments, difficulties in maintaining healthy interpersonal relationships, whether they be of a romantic nature or involve friends and family members, a preoccupation with self-centered conversations that neglect the opinions or perspectives of others, and a general indifference towards extending assistance to underprivileged individuals.

Prior to progressing further, it is essential that you gain a comprehensive understanding of Narcissistic Personality Disorder. It is imperative to ensure a comprehensive grasp of the concept of narcissistic abuse and how it intersects with other manifestations of abuse.

It is equally essential to understand that assigning the diagnosis of Narcissistic Personality Disorder to your mother is not within your purview. Indeed, should your mother not have officially received a medical diagnosis for the disorder, it would be inappropriate to assert that she is afflicted with said disorder. The sole individual with the authority to properly diagnose your mother with this condition is a licensed psychologist or psychiatrist. Nevertheless, acquiring knowledge about the disorder will enable you to gain a comprehensive understanding of narcissism as a whole. Determining whether your mother exhibits narcissistic traits can be discerned easily; however, it does not necessarily imply that she meets the precise criteria for a clinical diagnosis of narcissistic personality disorder.

At this juncture, you may experience ambivalent emotions towards your mother. One may experience discomfort upon becoming aware that she is plagued by an unrefined trait of her character which she has not yet acquired the skills to manage. Nonetheless, it is possible that you may experience anger upon the realization that you have endured narcissistic abuse and emerged as a survivor. Although the term "victim" is employed in this publication, it is of equal significance that you acknowledge yourself as a survivor, rather than primarily identifying as a victim.

Do not perceive it as necessary to simultaneously process all of your emotions. Indeed, it is likely to require several months to meticulously navigate through the complexities of your emotions. Please allocate an appropriate amount of time to process any emotions that may arise, as this is an integral component of your healing process. Engaging in the simulation of emotions will not facilitate the process of healing.

It is equally important to bear in mind the necessity of persisting in one's reading. You may encounter certain passages in this book that could present a challenge, as they may evoke recollections of your formative years. In the event of such occurrence, it is advised to pause momentarily and engage in a recreational activity before resuming the reading of this book.

Exploitation is prevalent

In the contemporary era, it proves arduous to navigate the challenges associated with possessing empathic abilities. In contemporary society, the world is characterized by its unrelenting, frigid, and ruthless nature. However, it is also remarkable and astounding, and the essential point is to not disregard the positive aspects when we feel overwhelmed by the negative. While not every individual possesses the quality of empathy, it would be advantageous for each of us to have some means of shielding ourselves from the emotional turmoil prevalent in today's society.

Show Consideration for the Messages Your Body is Conveying

The majority of contemporary medication revolves around the act of inducing relaxation in the body. We hear how we need to push through the agony and keep on in any event, when we are depleted. We consume supplements or ingest synthetic compounds, such as caffeine, with the intention of suppressing, masking, or altering the bodily signals that our system is attempting to communicate. We may perceive this as being pertinent periodically. Nonetheless, it frequently proves to be an error. Pain, distress, irritability, chronic illness, and fatigue are indicative signs that your body and mind have reached a point of depletion. Make an effort to avoid disregarding them. It is necessary to allocate time when required and learn to effectively decline requests. This is often the principal obstacle faced by empaths; it is exceedingly challenging to turn people down when we are aware of our ability to help. However, it is important to acknowledge that one's worth diminishes if personal well-being is compromised. One must address oneself before engaging with others.

Strive to minimize the usage of an excessive quantity of synthetic compounds or sweeteners.

Frequently, being an empath entails the management of excessive stimulation. Artificial compounds such as caffeine, additives, artificial colorants, and sweeteners can exacerbate hyperstimulation, thereby precipitating anxiety and other ailments. Eliminate the consumption of caffeine and sugar to the greatest extent feasible.

Ensure Sufficient Rest.

This seems to be a straightforward decision; how many individuals among us truly obtain sufficient rest? Insufficiently resting is often regarded as inconsequential. Nevertheless, it has been shown to have a comparable effect on your body akin to a blood alcohol concentration of 0.05. This hampers response time, impacts precision in tasks, induces irritability, and amplifies the extent to which things affect us. To effectively cope with the challenges presented by the world, it is imperative for empaths to ensure optimal functioning of all faculties, therefore it is advisable to prioritize sufficient rest. How would you determine that you have obtained an adequate amount of rest? Your physical well-being shall serve as an indicator of the situation.

Meditate

We frequently encounter this to an excessive degree. In general, the benefits of reflection are immeasurable. Research has provided evidence that contemplation is equally or even more effective than psychiatric medications in addressing anxiety, depression, and various other conditions. It can be challenging to undertake initially, particularly given our society's limited attention spans. However, persisting in our efforts is undoubtedly worthwhile. Irrespective of any absence of perceived events during the act of rumination, it is pertinent to acknowledge that both the cognitive and physiological aspects of your being are deriving benefits from this process of relaxation. Over time, the discernable improvements resulting from this practice shall become evident.

Please keep in mind the importance of showing gratitude" "Kindly remember to express appreciation" "It is important to be grateful" "Do not forget to demonstrate appreciation

This particular matter is more intricate than it might initially seem. Take into account: On a given day, how often do you genuinely experience feelings of gratitude? How frequently do you express gratitude for your possessions, or conversely, only acknowledge the value of your existence? It can be exceedingly challenging to recollect advantageous matters when we are consistently inundated with hostility from various sources. It is extensively pervasive, and we can indeed be easily ensnared by despondency if we fail to remind ourselves of the existence of goodness within our midst. There are several alternative manners in which this idea may be articulated using a formal tone: - One can pursue uncomplicated methods such as conducting a search for instances featuring individuals mutually assisting each other, consistently documenting five elements deserving of gratitude and expressing them vocally in the presence of others, aiding individuals who are less fortunate (note the contagious nature of appreciation), and recalling occasions when personal circumstances were less fortunate and how they were subsequently transformed. - A straightforward way to accomplish this entails conducting a thorough search for accounts of individuals engaging in acts of mutual assistance, diligently recording a list of five things to be thankful for on a regular basis, vocalizing this list for all to hear, proactively assisting those who are less fortunate (as gratitude tends to have a contagious effect), and consciously reflecting upon past instances of adversity and the subsequent improvements made. - To address this matter in a formal manner, one may opt for uncomplicated approaches such as researching accounts of individuals engaged in acts of mutual assistance, consistently documenting a list of five things to express gratitude for, verbalizing them openly, providing assistance to those less fortunate (considering that gratitude tends to have a contagious impact), and actively recalling moments of personal adversity, along with their subsequent transformations. There are such a significant number of things to be thankful for in this life. Remember any of them.

Allow Yourself to be Astonished

We frequently underestimate various aspects in life; yet, upon genuine contemplation, numerous of them prove to be truly awe-inspiring. Every object, ranging from the tiniest circle to the intricacies of the human hand, possesses its own enchanting marvel. How regularly do you consider it?

Reconnect with the Great Outdoors

One possible rephrasing in a formal tone could be: "Arguably, the primary impetus compelling individuals nowadays stems from the fact that they are leading lives incongruent with their inherent nature." Humans were not created with the purpose of laboring, taking breaks, and eventually perishing. We are impressively, impeccably, remarkably intricate sentient beings endowed with an immense capacity for behavior and emotion. We lead a lifestyle that deviates from that of our ancestors, and making an effort to reconnect with it proves highly advantageous for the mind, physique, and spirit. Put the telephone down. Mood killer the TV. Take a walk. Go outdoors. Embrace the practice of being barefoot! You might already be familiar with the concept of "earthing," which entails walking sans footwear on the ground in an effort to connect and harmonize with your body. There exists a comprehensive scientific framework underlying this phenomenon, and it engenders a profound sense of satisfaction under all circumstances. (This process is also referred to as "grounding" in relation to the electrical systems within your body, and grounding is crucial for empaths to engage in.) Indulge in a refreshing breath of fresh air and genuinely afford yourself the chance to embrace life for a period of time. You will be truly amazed by the significant difference it can make.

Envisioning Personal Security

Should you find yourself in a situation that seems overwhelming, whether it involves being surrounded by a large number of people or dealing with an emotionally draining individual, the most reliable form of defense lies within the realm of your own mind. Individuals with empathic abilities and sensitive dispositions possess an innate capacity to absorb the fervent energies emitted by others, akin to a highly receptive antenna. This can render the task of being in the vicinity of large crowds of individuals arduous, draining, and even daunting or unnerving. The optimal strategy to overcome it is to impede the accumulation of this energy. Prior to immersing yourself in the situation, make a conscious effort to pause and envision the flow of energy being impeded. One may conceptualize an impermeable barrier or airspace encompassing oneself, impeding the passage of energy. One may envision a reception mechanism retracting itself back into the depths of one's mind, rendering it incapable of receiving emotional input from others any longer. One can envision a scenario where an entranceway is firmly closed, effectively obstructing any entry into the recesses of one's mind, akin to a cord being disconnected or a section being severed. Regardless of which perception is presented to you, you have the ability to make use of it and it will prove effective.

There is no erroneous approach to accomplish this. Acquiring the necessary skills to manage it may require a certain degree of training; nevertheless, what is of paramount importance is the steadfastness of the perception. If you currently find yourself in this particular situation and experience a sense of being overwhelmed, you have the option to either seek a tranquil environment to accomplish the task or alternatively, concentrate diligently in your current location. The process is brief, and immediate relief can be experienced through the alleviation of the burden of others' intellectual capacity.

Develop the ability to decline requests politely.

This bears rehashing. Please be reminded that you have no obligation to anyone. It is evident that our purpose as empaths is to be entrusted with the task of assisting others. This should not be construed to mean that it is incumbent upon us to assist individuals with our own limitations. Individuals with narcissistic tendencies and other parasitic individuals are drawn to those with empathic qualities. They target us due to our resemblance to clairvoyant power sources, and they persistently drain our energy until we are depleted, unless we take preventive action to restrain their efforts. Assisting individuals is never intended to be a burden. Be attuned to your own being and acknowledge when that moment arrives.

In the present era, it proves to be challenging to be a person who possesses empathetic qualities; nonetheless, the sense of fulfillment derived from this characteristic is remarkable. By devising methods to establish stability and ensure personal safety, individuals are enhancing their own livelihoods along with the wellbeing of those they are purportedly engaging with during their existence.

Seven Strategies for Empaths to Alleviate or Address

Individuals with heightened empathy or sensitive disposition often encounter a certain level of post-traumatic stress.

This is partly attributable to the fact that, over an extended period of time, their systems have become inundated with adrenaline due to tactile overload. Various factors contribute to this, including instances of neglect or abuse, as well as the feeling of being unseen or lacking emotional support within their familial relationships.

Premature harm can manifest in a variety of forms. Possible sources include:"

• Occasionally witnessing arguments between your parents or relatives. • Occasional instances of your parents or relatives engaging in disputes.

• Receiving repetitive verbal admonishments.

• Physical and mental abuse.

• Suffering from public humiliation or being purportedly criticized for exhibiting an overly sensitive demeanor.

• Being tormented.

Regardless, being exposed to significant and continual disturbances and disarray within the household can evoke unpleasant emotions. A perceptive young individual with a highly sensitive disposition can absorb a greater amount of stress than others typically would in such circumstances.

When empaths are exposed to early trauma or mistreatment, their developing sensory system may undergo lasting disruption, leading to a state of hypervigilance. They have the potential to demonstrate remarkable receptiveness towards their environment in order to mitigate risks and ensure their safety or enter a heightened state of vigilance. This heightened state of vigilance exerts a tremendous toll on individuals who possess empathic traits.

The Individual with Narcissistic Traits and the Individual with Empathetic Characteristics

Opposites attract. Nevertheless, the alliance between a narcissist and an empath is untenable. Narcissists consistently seek individuals whom they can exploit, and among such individuals, the empath is particularly advantageous to the narcissist, except, perhaps, for the codependent, whom we will discuss momentarily. Due to the heightened sensitivity and exceptional self-awareness of empaths, they are often singled out. The individual characterized as a narcissist lacks the capacity for empathetic understanding, while simultaneously harboring a profound desire for adulation. The empath, being attuned to this aspect, is able to discern and acknowledge it. The empath shall assume the emotions of the narcissist, thereby engendering a heightened sense of obligation within the empath to attend to the narcissist's requirements.

Empaths generally exhibit compassion, as they internalize the emotions surrounding them, which often motivates them to make choices aimed at guaranteeing the fulfillment of everyone's needs in their vicinity. This reasoning is logical from an evolutionary perspective. When considering the empath's heightened sensitivity to the emotions of others, it follows that the empath would naturally absorb and reflect those emotional states. Subsequently, it is logical for the empath to exert significant effort in ensuring the well-being of everyone in their surroundings.

When observing the presence of an empath alongside a narcissist, it is typically safe to infer that the empath is making an effort towards benevolent intentions, as their innate inclination is rooted in offering selflessly. By their inherent nature, they possess a strong inclination to show affection towards others and demonstrate a profound fondness for showering those individuals with an abundance of love. Regrettably, though, an issue arises when the narcissist becomes involved. The narcissist possesses an inherent inclination for exploitation, and when their path intersects with the empath who holds immense compassion, a myriad of complications arise. The individual with narcissistic tendencies will exploit opportunities due to their ability to do so. He will prioritize assuming control of the empath in order to derive sustenance from the abundant wellspring of empathy they possess.

Ultimately, the empath possesses various dimensions within their personality that render them an appealing object of interest for the narcissist:

• The empath's propensity for compassion: The empath's inclination towards compassion appears to be a primary reason why they are vulnerable to the narcissist's targeting. Due to the empath's profound sense of compassion, one can observe the resultant depletion of this quality when faced with the narcissist's draining behavior. The empath recognizes the profound inner wounds of the narcissist, thus prompting the empath to exhibit compassion in their actions. The empath subsequently endeavors to assist the narcissist in any available means, notably in the pursuit of emotional healing via affectionate care.

• The empath's aversion to conflict: The empath strongly dislikes engaging in conflict. It is frequently characterized by strong emotions and presents considerable challenges in terms of navigation. Because of this, the empath regularly will simply allow other people to have their way with her because she would rather avoid all of the overwhelming feelings that come along with the attempt to assert oneself.

Is it possible for an individual to display narcissistic traits?

Family Change?

The phenomenon of narcissism is such that each individual inhabiting this planet possesses a degree of narcissistic characteristics within them. Upon reflection, it becomes evident that a universal desire among individuals is to experience a sense of uniqueness and recognition, particularly in certain contexts, thereby revealing that inherent self-centered tendencies are part of human nature. Essentially, we are all endeavoring to distinguish ourselves and enact meaningful change that will have a significant impact on the world. Therefore, it can be established that narcissism does not qualify as a disorder. It is deemed a disorder solely when our narcissistic personality permeates every facet of our existence. Narcissism transforms into a personality disorder solely when individuals exhibit a deficiency in both emotional self-regulation and empathy comprehension. Examining narcissism in this manner is akin to examining individuals with a personality disorder, such as borderline personality disorder, or a mood disorder, such as anxiety and depression. Is it possible to effectively manage, provide assistance for, find a cure for, or potentially modify these conditions? Indeed, a substantial amount of effort, dedication, resilience, and genuine motivation are necessary in order to effectively embrace the guidance provided by experts, thus enabling personal growth and effective management of narcissistic tendencies. Similar to anxiety, in order to achieve improvement, it is imperative to modify various elements of one's lifestyle to effectively manage and cope with it. This includes making dietary adjustments and altering cognitive patterns, as well as refining one's response to worry and overall approach to life. Prescribed medication can effectively address the issue, however, in order to achieve a truly satisfying existence, it is imperative to invest the necessary efforts to overcome it, just as one would do with any mental or physical health condition.

In order for individuals with narcissistic tendencies to undergo genuine transformation, it is imperative that they develop a sense of ease in acquainting themselves with their own emotions at a profound level. This process enables them to unveil the deeply rooted feelings of shame and insecurity that lie beneath the surface. They must acquire the ability to undertake personal sacrifices within their own sphere, such as willingly relinquishing the limelight, exercising heightened mindfulness in their behavior to prioritize others, and overcoming their feelings of shame by requesting assistance. To elicit a desire for change in a narcissist, three elements must be presented: Leverage

In order to motivate the narcissist to seek therapy or even contemplate the idea of therapy, a certain form of leverage must be employed. This may encompass apprehension regarding the potential loss of a loved one, the possibility of job termination or loss of authority, or the jeopardy of their social standing and reputation.

A method of therapy" or "A treatment strategy

Similar to how cognitive behavioral therapy (CBT) has shown efficacy in addressing anxiety conditions, and dialectical behavior therapy (DBT) has proven beneficial for individuals with borderline personality disorder, it is important for those with narcissistic tendencies to seek an appropriate therapeutic approach tailored to their specific needs. Schema therapy could be an effective therapeutic intervention for individuals with narcissistic tendencies as it targets the underlying cognitive patterns and revisits the emotional narrative within the brain.

A competent counsellor

A competent therapist is an individual who avoids developing attachments or being easily swayed. The ideal therapist for individuals with narcissistic tendencies is someone who is adept at avoiding behaviors that may provoke the narcissistic tendencies, while also being skilled at establishing firm limits and boundaries. This approach would involve the therapist adopting a mentality of "parenting" the vulnerable aspect of the narcissist's psyche, all the while ensuring their responsibility for their thoughts and behaviors. Once the ideal psychologist has been located, they will proceed to instruct the narcissist on the methods of transformation. The modification will have the following appearance:

• Imparting insight into the correlation between one's actions and the resultant negative emotions and thoughts (or vice versa)

• Imparting to the narcissist a comprehensive understanding of the potential repercussions arising from these involuntary cognitions and emotions, thereby compelling them to assume full accountability for their every action.

• Providing the narcissist with the perception of autonomy, wherein they believe that their decisions shape their outcome in addressing their abusive tendencies.

- Amidst feelings of anger, sadness, loneliness, and other similar emotions. has the capacity to instruct the narcissist in developing self-awareness regarding the underlying causes of their distress, thereby enabling them to adopt alternative courses of action that diverge from their initial emotional responses

As evident, the endeavor of facilitating a narcissist's transformation holds significant magnitude. However, should a narcissist remain in a state of denial regarding the existence of a problem, they will be incapable of acknowledging their shortcomings and instead choose to persist unabated on their current trajectory. One issue with this situation is the inherent peril of engaging in disputes and conflicts with a narcissistic individual. This undertaking can prove dangerously precarious for the target, given the complex psychological nature of the narcissist's actions that often leave the victim perplexed and unable to comprehend their motives. If you openly accuse them of being narcissistic, the individuals' heightened susceptibility to criticism could potentially harm you to a greater extent than your critique affects their self-esteem (How to Handle a Person with Narcissistic Characteristics, 2018).

A Group of Individuals Exhibiting Narcissistic Traits

When discussing narcissism within the family, we are not solely referring to a single individual displaying narcissistic behavior. The presence of narcissistic tendencies or traits can exert a wide-ranging influence on the entire familial unit, as being a narcissistic parent inherently predisposes one to raise their child in a narcissistic manner. In the event that there is a child displaying narcissistic tendencies, it is highly likely that within the family dynamic, there will exist an individual who consistently rationalizes and justifies the child's behavior. Unfortunately, this inadvertently reinforces the child's narcissistic traits, further cementing their presence and influence.

This could have a significant impact on every occasion spent collectively, transforming a simple afternoon with your relatives into a memorable disaster.

Allow me to elaborate on the ramifications of narcissism that encompass the entire family unit.

The category of individuals fulfilling this role encompasses the marital partner of a narcissistic individual, the maternal or paternal grandmother of a narcissistic offspring, or a near kin.

The facilitator facilitates the narcissist's conduct by rationalizing their behaviors in order to mitigate additional disagreement.

The Flying Monkey: These individuals, encompassing any person, are commonly portrayed as agents of the narcissist who inflict harm upon the other members. For instance, in a particular scenario, an adult sibling may have terminated their communication with the narcissistic sibling, and if the parent assumes the role of the flying monkey, they may instill feelings of shame and guilt within the sister for severing those connections.

• The Scapegoat: This individual within the family assumes the role of candidly identifying the narcissistic individual as they truly are - someone afflicted with Narcissistic Personality Disorder (NPD). They prefer to state the truth rather than excessively flattering the narcissist and giving them undue attention. Typically, such conduct tends to elicit disapproval from the rest of the familial unit, as they perceive the scapegoat's lack of support towards the narcissist as unconstructive.

• The Cherished Offspring: Typically, this refers to an offspring of a parent with narcissistic tendencies, who receives a disproportionate amount of admiration and attention compared to their siblings or peers. This leads to discord among other members of the family, as the favored child may serve as a mechanism for assigning blame or manipulating others within the familial unit.

Frequently, the status of the favored offspring can be altered when they express dissent or distance themselves from the idolized perception held by their parent, leading the parent to engage in abusive behavior and manipulate their own child psychologically (How to Handle a Narcissist, 2018).

These familial characteristics may contribute to chaotic holiday gatherings and necessitate a collective effort from the family to instigate change. Although it may be a significant undertaking for a solitary individual to undergo transformation, to ensure the collective cooperation and willingness of the entire family, it would be imperative to establish specific therapeutic elements accompanied by a structured framework delineating the projected course of events. Moreover, it is imperative that it caters to individuals across the board;

failure to do so could lead to the complete disintegration of the project, exacerbating the characteristics associated with narcissism.

Narcissistic Holidays

On family holidays, there are two potential scenarios: either the individual displaying narcissistic tendencies abstains from attending, or their presence at the gathering gives rise to an atmosphere of tension. Festivals like Christmas, birthdays, Thanksgiving, New Year's, and so on. has the potential to incite bursts of rage and tantrums due to the narcissistic tendencies and perfectionistic proclivities. The endeavor to derive pleasure from the holiday season extends beyond the narcissist's personal sphere and permeates the lives of the victims, particularly in instances where the narcissist has effectively achieved the isolation of their victim. In the event that an individual has recently terminated a relationship or ceased communication with a narcissistic individual, particularly if their identity was centered around pleasing the narcissist as a means of evading their anger, manipulative tactics, and attempts to attribute blame, a sense of emptiness may arise during the holiday season. Arguably, the most arduous aspect of progressing with one's life is the endeavor to redefine one's identity in light of the relentless liberation from perpetual self-sacrifice and devotion to a narcissistic individual.

Holidays, on the other hand, offer an opportune time for regaining one's composure (in the absence of the narcissist). They afford the opportunity to reestablish connections with one's family, partake in nourishing dietary habits, and reconstruct relationships with individuals of an encouraging and optimistic nature, with whom one had previously maintained strong ties. In addition to reestablishing connections, it is crucial to ensure that you prioritize self-care during the upcoming festive season. Consider attending to your well-being in a manner akin to tending to the needs of your offspring if they were afflicted with melancholy or any other ailment of the heart. Engage in physical activity, prioritize adequate rest, maintain proper hydration, nurture yourself, embrace affirmations that foster self-assurance, and so forth. There are additional actions you can undertake this holiday season to elevate your emotional well-being following a narcissistic wound, such as:

1. Exercise self-restraint and maintain composure in dealing with oneself.

One should not anticipate an immediate ability to progress, nor should one anticipate an immediate experience of happiness. One may experience a sense of alleviation, only for the recollections of shared moments during holiday seasons to evoke the emotions of bliss once again. Pursue actions that bring you joy while acknowledging that perfection is not obligatory, nor is utter failure. Should you not feel inclined to participate in the festivities this year, I encourage you to grant yourself additional time, as there is no obligation to engage in activities that do not align with your desires.

2. Embrace the opportunity to reconstruct what has been lost. Which traditions did you previously partake in prior to the arrival of the narcissist in your life? Was it observing the festive holiday illuminations? Did you dress up for Halloween? Could it be attributed to

expressing gratitude via assisting an individual who required assistance? It is advisable to persist in the activities in question, as the narcissist has not managed to tarnish these particular 63 endeavors.

yet. If you choose not to pursue your past endeavors, then you alone bear responsibility for their cessation.

3. Identify individuals who exhibit toxic traits and proactively distance yourself from them. Familiarize yourself with those who display unsupportive behavior in your pursuits, as their presence will hinder your progress in the journey of personal growth. Conduct a thorough analysis of your acquaintances, relatives, and associations to ascertain the individuals who remain supportive and those who may not be. Which individuals have your best interests at heart, and which merely

exploit you for their own ulterior motives. It is advisable to steer clear of individuals who exhibit toxic behavior, if possible, and instead, actively seek the company of those who are non-toxic, in order to enhance the quality of time spent with others.

4. Provide, provide, provide

It is empirically demonstrated that when we engage in acts of generosity, our brains release endorphin hormones, often referred to as the 'feel good' hormone. Contributing to other individuals through the act of making donations, assisting an individual in unloading their groceries, or imparting one's knowledge to provide guidance are all methods by which one may extend generosity to others, thus evoking a sense of personal satisfaction. Additional concepts incorporate the removal of refuse from public thoroughfares, the cultivation of vegetation, or offering one's services in aid of shelters for both humans and animals.

The absence of the narcissist during the holidays brings about a level of unfamiliarity that poses challenges to one's ability to derive enjoyment from the festive season. Once you initiate the practice of solitude and self-care, you will observe an improvement in the forthcoming days, and ultimately, you will find amusement in your own actions as you gradually release yourself from the grasp of the oppressor. Take pleasure in the relief from the burden and pressure caused by their presence, and make sure to maintain a demeanor of empathy towards both yourself and others.

Narcissists take great pleasure in holidays, primarily due to the increased opportunity it provides for them to bask in attention and showcase their inflated sense of superiority, overshadowing others in their constant pursuit of validation. They have a penchant for exerting control, engaging in conflicts, and seeking attention. What better way to express one's sense of pride and accomplishment than by declaring it unabashedly during the festive period? I have previously examined the notion of holidays proceeding in the absence of the narcissist. However, what course of action should be undertaken if the narcissist continues to be present during a holiday? Presented here is an illustrative depiction of what a holiday gathering might entail when a narcissistic individual is included within the familial context.

The meticulous hand of the curator.

From the meticulously adorned Christmas tree to the elaborately embellished front yard on Halloween, and in the splendid spectacle of the most spectacular fireworks display on New Year's, holidays afford the narcissist an opportunity to flaunt their accomplishments and vie for superiority among their peers. Should you receive an invitation, please be advised that the hosts will assume responsibility for all arrangements. However, in the event that you are not included, rest assured that they will make a point to share their accomplishments via social media and inform you through text messaging.

Exploitation of the act of gift-giving

Given their proclivity for engaging in manipulative tactics and seeking to exert control over others, the holiday season presents narcissists with an opportune occasion to indulge in both of these behaviors. For instance, in the context of a Christmas gathering involving gift exchange, the narcissist not only seeks to flaunt their own presents, but also explicitly conveys to others that their gifts surpass or will surpass those of others. In the event that you receive a gift from the individual with narcissistic tendencies, rather than experiencing pleasure, you will endure the challenging consequences."

The considerable exertion they had to undergo in acquiring that particular gift for you. They will, in some manner, shift the focus of the gift-giving scenario towards themselves, emphasizing the gratitude they expect to receive for their diligent efforts to acquire something that they believed symbolized you. Allocating gifts towards the narcissist is solely centered on their own personal gratification and not concerned with others.

The necessity for regulation

Have you ever observed or been involved in a situation where one child is favored more than the others, or in the absence of siblings, where one individual is preferred over everyone else? This is the methodology employed by the narcissist to assert dominance and exert control in a given scenario. When they exhibit bias towards one individual while singling out another, they are inviting scrutiny and criticism. This situation often gives rise to conflict since, in numerous instances, one finds themselves within the narcissist's premises, thereby leading to the remark, "If you are dissatisfied, please vacate the premises."

The self-centered parent

This occurrence does not exclusively need to transpire solely during holiday gatherings; as it has been previously elucidated within this chapter, there is consistently an individual who assumes the role of the family's 'scapegoat.' In conclusion, the individual who espouses the unvarnished truth.

Nevertheless, this individual consistently bears the brunt of adversity or mistreatment due to their inherent qualities. The remaining children rally in support of their self-centered mother in order to avoid experiencing mistreatment or humiliation when expressing a differing perspective than her, which is commonly known as gaslighting. The scapegoat, on the other hand, assumes the role of the "

The 'black sheep' is subject to condemnation not only from the mother but also from the entire family due to the critical nature of the 'goat.' In contrast, while the scapegoat is ostracized or distinguished, the remaining family members conform to the mother's perspective and adopt her ways, as this is the societal framework in which they were raised.

Please bear in mind that this is the method employed in the context of narcissistic abuse to terminate the relationship.

Although holidays are intended to be enjoyable, their overall experience is often marred when overseen by or involving an individual with narcissistic tendencies. The most effective approach to handling a holiday that entails the presence of individuals with narcissistic tendencies is to derive satisfaction from the occasion, exhibit patience towards such individuals, and subsequently minimize contact with them for an extended period, all the while making improved decisions and carving out a fulfilling life for oneself. With that being said, is it possible for a family with narcissistic traits to undergo transformation? As you have acquired knowledge on this matter, indeed, it is possible for them to do so, albeit requiring a significant exertion of effort and labor. It is imperative that the cycle be interrupted so as to dismantle the sway of narcissism.

Take Control Back

The detrimental effects of emotional abuse are profound, and failing to undergo the process of healing increases one's susceptibility to engaging in similar types of relationships. You have undergone psychological harm and will likely encounter symptoms such as anxiety, depression, dissociation, feelings of diminished self-esteem, reduced self-worth, distressing dreams, and recurring memories. It is imperative that you pursue therapeutic guidance to facilitate your recuperation; nonetheless, there are tactics you can integrate into your routine that will aid you in progressing.

Yoga

The consequences of trauma are present in the body, and yoga is a practice that integrates physical movement and mindfulness to establish and restore equilibrium. Studies have demonstrated that yoga effectively mitigates feelings of anxiety and depression, ameliorates symptoms associated with post-traumatic stress disorder in individuals who have experienced domestic violence, enhances self-confidence, and enhances perceptions of one's own physical appearance. Yoga comprises a sequence of potent physical exercises aimed at addressing the inherent sense of powerlessness experienced by survivors of abuse.

Dr. Bessel Van der Kolk has devoted considerable time to researching the advantages of yoga, and he maintains that it enables individuals who have experienced trauma to regain agency over their physical selves. Trauma deprives individuals who have undergone abuse of a feeling of security, and the practice of yoga assists them in reestablishing this connection by harnessing bodily sensations.

Meditation

The occurrence of trauma has the potential to disturb the neural region responsible for memory retention, cognitive development, emotional management, and strategic thinking. Studies have revealed that meditation elicits positive effects on the aforementioned brain regions that are implicated in trauma, namely the hippocampus, amygdala, and prefrontal cortex. Meditation gives abuse victims their psyche back. It facilitates neuroregeneration and enables individuals to approach life with a sense of empowerment rather than being constrained by the ramifications of past traumas.

Engaging in a regular practice of meditation enhances the connectivity of neural circuits within the brain and augments the density of grey matter in regions associated with both the fight or flight reaction and the regulation of emotions. Additionally, meditation enables you to gain consciousness regarding your inclination to establish communication with the individual who caused harm. When the victims lack awareness of this fact, they tend to make impulsive choices that often result in their eventual return to the relationship. It further enhances your overall emotional awareness.

Anchor Yourself

Typically, individuals who have endured emotional abuse have been subjected to the manipulation tactic of gaslighting, wherein they are induced to believe that the abuse they have suffered is a product of their own imagination. It is crucial for you to firmly establish a connection with the reality that you have endured abuse, while also recognizing that you are currently outside of that harmful environment. It is a prevailing tendency among individuals who have experienced abuse to romanticize the relationship they were involved in and contemplate hypothetical scenarios wherein they possessed the ability to satisfy their partner. Engaging with actuality is also beneficial when grappling with ambivalent sentiments toward the individual who has caused you harm. As previously stated, one of the tactics employed by narcissists is to exhibit affection and subsequently retract it, and it is the loving disposition of the narcissist that attracts individuals who become victimized. The narcissist endeavors to undermine the victim's perception of reality, yet upon regaining a connection with one's own reality, the true nature of the perpetrator becomes apparent.

After leaving an abusive relationship, survivors become highly susceptible to manipulation by their abusers, who often resort to demonstrating affection and kindness to entice them into returning. It is imperative that you prohibit incoming phone calls, text messages, and any other means of communication to ensure that he does not have the opportunity to infiltrate your thoughts. This enables you to establish a connection with the actual occurrence concerning you, as opposed to permitting him to persuade you that your perception of the events is erroneous.

To commence the initiation of anchoring, compile a catalog of ten of the most egregious occurrences that transpired within the context of your previous romantic affiliation. When the inclination arises to reestablish contact with your abuser, we recommend perusing this inventory and redirecting your thoughts towards reminiscing on his malevolence towards you, his degradation of your being, and the manner in which he compelled you to feel decidedly subhuman. In addition, you may choose to document sentiments regarding the emotional impact inflicted upon you, such as: "My perpetrator engendered in me a sense of worthlessness." "My perpetrator induced feelings of profound melancholy." "My perpetrator instilled in me a sense of intellectual inadequacy."

"My perpetrator reinforced the belief that I deserved mistreatment and that no one could ever provide the same level of affection as they did." It is advisable to recall these emotions whenever the temptation arises to initiate contact via phone or visit their residence. Consider reflecting on whether it is emotionally beneficial for someone to manipulate your perception of yourself in this manner. The greater capacity you have to recall the adverse emotions linked with the relationship, the more effortless it will become to maintain your distance.

Engage in Emotional Regulation Techniques with Your Inner Child

You did not merely encounter an abusive relationship by chance, but rather, you are facing this situation due to underlying, ingrained factors within you that have shaped your life, often originating from your childhood.

Through therapeutic intervention, you will come to realize that certain intrinsic needs were left unfulfilled in your formative years. In your endeavor to address that emptiness, you ultimately acquiesced to a relationship characterized by abusive dynamics. After identifying the void, it is crucial to acquire an understanding of what is necessary to alleviate it, in order to safeguard yourself from entering into another detrimental relationship. Throughout the process of healing, it is imperative to exhibit profound self-compassion due to the traumatic experiences of your childhood, bearing in mind that the mistreatment you have suffered is by no means a reflection of your own wrongdoing. Mistreatment possesses the capability to resurface previously unresolved emotional traumas. The conviction that you have perpetually harbored an inadequate self-perception has ingrained itself within the depths of your subconscious. Your partner who engages in abusive behavior has merely reaffirmed the longstanding sentiments you have harbored. During the process of healing, it is crucial to alter the discourse occurring within your thoughts, a matter of great significance particularly when recuperating from instances of abuse. Self-compassion possesses great potential for being the most potent manifestation of empathy; hence, it is crucial to exercise gentleness towards oneself amidst this period.

When you begin experiencing these adverse emotions, console yourself in a manner akin to offering solace to a child who is subjected to harassment in the recreational area. Convince yourself that you embody the exact opposite characteristics of what the negative self-talk is attempting to instill in your mind.

Expressions that you may employ include, "One may make affirmations like, 'I possess inherent value,' 'I possess unique qualities,' 'I am deserving of favorable circumstances in my existence.' Gradually, one shall acquire the ability to relinquish self-reproach and emerge victorious over the deleterious burden of shame imposed upon them." When engaging in self-evaluation of the events, there is an increased likelihood of giving in to self-defeating actions. However, you can alleviate this by exhibiting self-compassion and affirming your inherent worthiness of self-kindness and self-care.

Exercise

Incorporating physical activity into your daily schedule, such as engaging in extended walks, jogging, enrolling in dance classes, or becoming a member at a fitness center, can greatly contribute to the process of recovery. In the absence of motivation, it is advisable not to overwhelm yourself with excessive tasks. Instead, it may be beneficial to commence with a brief ten-minute stroll, gradually progressing and extending the duration over time. Physical activity decreases cortisol levels and triggers the release of endorphins, thereby enabling the replacement of the biochemical dependence that has been formed with your abuser with a constructive and beneficial alternative. This addiction has been engendered by the influence of chemical substances such as cortisol, dopamine, serotonin, and adrenaline, which amplify the attachment to the perpetrator and establish a pattern of alternating states of euphoria and despair. Engaging in physical activity enables the development of a foundation of fortitude and endurance subsequent to departing from an abusive situation. Additionally, it aids in mitigating numerous physiological issues commonly associated with abuse, including but not limited to, excessive weight gain, sleep disturbances, premature aging, and compromised immune function.

Eliminate Unhealthy Coping Strategies

You made every conceivable effort to ensure the contentment of your narcissistic partner and prevent any outbursts of anger. Your days were consumed by an existence riddled with caution and trepidation. You acquired the skill of maintaining a stance of reticence and docility, scrutinizing each action you took and commencing every conversation with the phrase, "I apologize." You became adept at evading conflicts and navigating treacherous terrain, pretending as though certain aspects of your aspirations, wishes, and necessities were nonexistent. You acquired the ability to undervalue your own worth and tolerate mistreatment from another individual in a manner that is utterly unacceptable. The emotional torment you endured in order to attain a modicum of tranquility and safeguard yourself, and potentially your offspring, from peril was truly remarkable. These distressing lessons you have acquired are not just detrimental, but they also lack utility in a conventional relationship. As a result, it is imperative that you acquire fresh and conventional patterns that will prove advantageous in a wholesome relationship. The process of relinquishing old habits necessitates a framework of self-observation, comprising two distinct forms: qualitative and quantitative.

Monitoring for Quality: This entails attentively observing the recurring patterns of behavior you engage in—taking note of their appearance and impact on your emotional state.

Quantitative Surveillance: This entails tracking the frequency of obsolete behavioral patterns to ascertain the frequency at which they occur within your daily routine.

While both forms of self-monitoring demonstrate efficacy, quantitative monitoring stands out as particularly advantageous due to its ability to provide accurate measurements of behavior and identify the underlying triggers that give rise to these detrimental patterns. Formerly, you might have possessed a rudimentary comprehension of the severity of your predicament, but presently you have attained the ability to effectively discern and quantify your progress.

It is imperative to implement a standardized framework for the process of self-monitoring. It is imperative to encompass the elements under scrutiny, establish the methodology for documenting observations, and delineate the frequency at which the monitoring process will be conducted. Take, for instance, a prevalent coping mechanism adopted by women trapped in an abusive relationship, wherein they tend to rationalize and accept the abusive behavior as normal. This behavior is achieved through the process of self-persuasion, where individuals justify the mistreatment by convincing themselves that they merit such treatment. Additionally, they may rationalize their experiences by reinforcing the notion that other women also encounter similar circumstances, implying that this conduct is customary for men. It is unfeasible to closely observe and track every thought that occurs within one's mind. At times, individuals may be unaware that they are engaging in such thoughts on a conscious level. Nevertheless, there will be instances when you become aware of the information, and it is during these moments that you should document the data. There is no necessity for complexity in this process; one only needs to maintain a notebook at hand and record the information. In the event that you become aware of any underlying cause that prompted you to initiate such thought processes, it is advisable to duly document it as well. Kindly record the respective date, time, reflection, catalyst, and initial emotional state associated with the onset of these thoughts.

Cultivate self-acceptance and self-compassion

While this statement may appear trite, it is of utmost importance to progress in one's life and ultimately cultivate a wholesome romantic relationship. When one nurtures self-love, one gains profound self-awareness and a steadfast conviction in their values. It is impossible for anyone to come along and try to convince you that you are anything less than the best! When you develop a certain level of confidence and self-worth, nothing can shake you. Outlined below are several suggestions on cultivating self-love following the experience of an abusive relationship.

Attain Physical Fitness: A well-toned physique not only enhances physical well-being, but also contributes to an improved sense of self-esteem. As we have previously explored the advantageous effects of regular physical activity, achieving a desirable appearance serves as an additional advantage. Deliberate upon not solely enhancing your well-being, but undergoing a complete metamorphosis of your physical form. Strive to achieve the weight and physique aligned with your personal ideals.

Revamp Your Attire: Upon attaining your desired physique, reward yourself with a fresh selection of garments. There is no necessity to deplete your financial resources; rather, invest in iconic articles that will genuinely enhance your self-confidence.

Indulge in Solitary Pleasures: Set aside a designated day each week to engage in activities that bring you joy and fulfillment. Many individuals who have experienced abuse often struggle with solitude, rendering them vulnerable targets for perpetrators. Engaging in solitary activities cultivates the capacity to relish one's own presence. Possible alternatives: - Possible activities to consider may involve attending a film screening, dining out at a restaurant, or exploring a new recreational pursuit. - Some options that could be explored are attending a movie theater, dining at a restaurant, or discovering a fresh pastime. - You may wish to engage in activities such as watching a film, dining at an eatery, or taking up a new hobby. - Among the potential choices are going to see a movie, eating out at a restaurant, or pursuing a new leisure pursuit.

Engage in Novel Experiences: Explore activities outside of your usual repertoire. Engage in novel and exhilarating activities such as partaking in skydiving or bungee jumping. While the suggestion may appear somewhat excessive, as the ultimate arbiter of your own preferences and understanding of yourself, you have the autonomy to select something that will assuredly introduce a sense of astonishment into your existence.

Embark on a Vacation: Even if you do not establish it as a customary practice, make it a point to indulge in a vacation at a certain destination. Travel to a nation that is radically outside your sphere of familiarity. If you are lacking the necessary courage to embark on this journey individually, I would recommend extending an invitation to a companion. Immerse oneself in a distinct cultural milieu, indulge in novel culinary exploits, partake in a diverse array of activities, and derive enjoyment from the experience.

Document: Documenting your thoughts and feelings in a personal journal can serve as a constructive outlet for releasing any lingering negative emotions. Additionally, it is an effective method for monitoring and evaluating your personal development. Upon exiting an abusive relationship, it is probable that the number of negative days experienced will surpass those of a positive nature. Certain days will exhibit more favorable conditions, yet as time elapses, you will discern a gradual establishment of emotional equilibrium.

Acquire the Ability to Deny: The act of submission serves as a means of self-preservation for women involved in abusive partnerships. One would never be inclined to refuse or decline a request from one's partner, apprehensive of the potential consequences that may ensue. Nevertheless, given that you are no longer caught in an abusive relationship, it is imperative that you refrain from carrying over this submissiveness into your friendships, and resist the impulse to appease others by always responding affirmatively. This will deplete your energy and encroach upon your personal time.

Acknowledge Your Achievements: Regardless of how trivial you perceive the accomplishment to be, make a point to commemorate it. Successfully navigating an entire day without dwelling on thoughts of your former partner constitutes an achievement, just as maintaining a steadfast commitment to your daily exercise regimen embodies an accomplishment. Please take note of these matters and take proper care of yourself in relation to them.

Engage in Personal Experimentation: Is there any pursuit or aspiration that you have long harbored but have yet to actively pursue? Create a comprehensive inventory of these tasks and commence their execution. You might have harbored a lifelong aspiration to participate in a triathlon or to acquire supplementary credentials. Make a resolute determination to accomplish any goal upon which you set your mind.

Embrace Self-Reliance: Prior to entering into an abusive relationship, your intuitive faculties indicated an unsettling notion that warranted caution. However, you consciously disregarded these signals, opting to pursue the relationship with the expectation that circumstances would improve. Acquaint yourself with that sensation, as it will be indicative of any instances where things are amiss, extending beyond just interpersonal relationships and encompassing various aspects of your existence.

A Species unto Themselves

Let us adopt a diplomatic approach and express that they possess a truly distinct quality. People frequently fail to comprehend the rationale behind the consistent fulfillment of desires exhibited by individuals with Narcissistic personality traits. They do not abide by rules or regulations; rather, they acquire what they desire, even resorting to coercion if necessary.

This is precisely the reason why they are seldom disturbed, and they exude an air of unwavering self-assurance. They possess a strong conviction in their ability to deftly orchestrate circumstances for their personal benefit. It is crucial to recognize that what you are observing is an insincere façade. An individual's creation, strongly self-sustained. The individual exhibiting narcissistic traits possesses identical anxieties to your own. They experience identical ailments, often with a heightened severity surpassing yours. The issue at hand is that they effectively conceal their fears by adamantly refusing to acknowledge them. They establish a mechanism by which they can disregard that fact for their own benefit.

Furthermore, they possess an exclusive approach to living their lives. Formulating their own perception of reality and fabricating the verifiable information while progressing through life. When drawing a comparison to anglers, they do not simply deploy a solitary hook but instead opt for a more extensive approach by casting a significantly broader net or dispersing chum in the water. They never show interest in an individual participant but instead adopt a perspective on life that encourages bringing more people together.

This attribute also ensures safety. If an option selected happens to be unsatisfactory, an alternative is readily available. When a number of individuals fail to meet the expectations, it does not significantly impact the overall outcome.

In more concise terms, their fishing practices lack specificity towards any particular species, instead encompassing a general approach. Any variety will suffice as they are all edible.

This elucidates their lack of emotional connection to any specific individual. It is never about you; it is never personal as much as you would like to believe it to be but only about what they get out of you. That would consequently imply that the pronoun "You" could encompass anyone who is inclined to furnish what they seek. Individuals do not form attachments to specific individuals, but rather to abstract notions such as affection, desire, wealth, or renown.

The individual who caters to this particular desire of theirs, while maintaining a non-judgmental and trouble-free approach, emerges victorious and earns the jackpot. With that being stated, it is crucial to highlight the fact that if you have recognized yourself as someone with a special interest in Narcissistic individuals, it is imperative for you to understand that you, as an individual, hold little significance to that person.

Nevertheless, what holds significant importance to them is precisely what they ardently desire, and if they acquire that from your association, it elucidates the reason behind their choice to be in your company. Provided that you continue to offer, they will retain their presence.

They harbor no affection towards you, and they do not find themselves in a realm where they cannot fathom a life without your presence. They have a strong affinity towards the offerings you provide, without question.

If that is truly the case, whereby one manages to elude any repercussions for their actions, it must be emphasized that you are facing grave consequences.

It is frequently quite challenging to alter a situation of that nature, I must admit. They would rather part ways with you than make alterations on your behalf. They will not exhibit the willingness to undergo a comprehensive transformation solely for your benefit. In order to locate the possessions they shared with you, venturing to a different location will undoubtedly present itself as a significantly more attainable endeavor.

As a parent, it perpetually astounds me how we consistently place high expectations on children throughout their lives. It is our anticipation that they will demonstrate proper usage of utensils, exhibit proficiency in utilizing the bathroom and its amenities, diligently complete their academic assignments, regularly tend to their own bed-making duties, and display respect towards their parents.

It is curious how we continuously fail to anticipate that our significant others would consistently exhibit basic courtesy and respect in their interactions with us. Furthermore, we place utmost importance on instilling in our children the value of displaying kindness under all circumstances.

This implies that in their adulthood, they are likely to tolerate all forms of undesirable conduct from others while maintaining a pleasant demeanor. These individuals are ideal targets for individuals with Narcissistic tendencies.

A significant portion of children are susceptible to this detrimental approach, which explains the presence of individuals with narcissistic traits who are able to evade accountability for their reprehensible actions. They became aware and acknowledged that they possessed the capabilities to exert influence over all others, leveraging the prevailing beliefs held by those others.

If you are on the verge of engaging with a Narcissistic scenario in your personal life, it is prudent to heed a note of caution. Exercise utmost caution in your actions and the methods you opt for.

Prior to making a decision, I kindly request that you carefully contemplate the individual repercussions and make a well-informed judgment accordingly. It is a perilous endeavor that can unfold in unpredictable ways. It is imperative that you are well-informed of this matter.

In addition, it is worth noting that individuals who engage in Narcissistic behaviors are under the belief that their actions are devoid of wrongdoing. However, they will perceive your lack of willingness to cooperate with their desires and requirements as the sole catalyst for all issues.

Do not succumb to the imposition of external rules or values; instead, maintain accountability to your own.

You will greatly benefit yourself by adopting such a position. It is essential to acknowledge that an individual with Narcissistic traits possesses a keen awareness of their own wrongdoings. The discrepancy lies in their lack of acknowledgment of the wrongdoing when engaging in such actions. It is indisputable that their lack of comprehension is not the issue at hand; rather, they strategically rely on the assumption that you will refrain from speaking up due to apprehensions about the impact on your own standing within the relationship.

Therefore, endorsing their conduct with your seal of approval.

They rely on the assumption that you possess a high level of dependency on them and that you will prioritize your personal safety above all else.

Ensuring their affinity towards you and the preservation of your presence.

Even when that necessitates relinquishing one's own needs and personal convictions.

Restoring the Confidence That Has Been Eroded.

1. Accepting The Abuse. Acceptance is regarded as one of the fundamental processes in the recovery journey. Hold the belief that your partner harbors harmful qualities, as it has adversely impacted your well-being, cognitive state, and self-worth. It is indeed acknowledged that you have not received the love that you rightfully deserved. Therefore, embarking on the process of mourning the individual who subjected you to prolonged mistreatment is an initial stride towards attaining healing and restoration.

Additionally, anger serves as an integral catalyst in facilitating your rejuvenation process. In order to effectively address the issue, we recommend you retrieve a notepad and meticulously compile a comprehensive inventory of your partner's actions. Please produce a maximum number of written responses. Title it: "Categorize as 'Undesirable Characteristics'." By consistently recognizing these traits, one can discern the maliciousness within an individual, rather than inflicting harm upon oneself. This ongoing awareness allows for a steadfast commitment to righteousness.

Additionally, consider expressing your frustration to the public, while refraining from adopting a chaotic demeanor. By voicing your concerns, you will further solidify your realization that you were manipulated. You may potentially encounter individuals who claim to have had prior knowledge, yet hesitated to disclose it. Furthermore, you could potentially offer assistance in preventing individuals from becoming victims of manipulation by a narcissistic individual.

2. Build a New Life. The impact of constructing a new life around oneself cannot be overstated. Commence establishing connections with individuals who are prepared to offer assistance during periods of difficulty. As you embark on a pursuit of a contemporary way of life, it is advisable to document the Attributes that are compatible within a romantic partnership (I have previously discussed the characteristics of a strong relationship). This will serve as a valuable reference point for you in navigating your romantic endeavors.

3. Reflect. Indeed, the more comprehensive your understanding of the events and their underlying causes, the greater the likelihood of avoiding manipulation by the Narcissist. Kindly record the events that transpired and document the distinguishing characteristics exhibited by the Narcissist in the initial stages of the relationship. This will serve as a directive to help you observe crimson markings and indications. Moreover, by observing from a distance, one can ascertain whether they are at risk of being exploited and then discarded at the conclusion of the relationship.

Are you equipped to effectively handle an individual with narcissistic tendencies? Tips and Strategies

What if one does not exhibit any codependent characteristics, but rather encounters individuals with narcissistic tendencies and must navigate interactions with them? It is possible that your colleague may exhibit narcissistic tendencies. It is also possible that your own employer exhibits narcissistic tendencies, an inherently nuanced and intricate situation. It is plausible that you may have a mother-in-law who exhibits narcissistic traits. Perhaps you have a desire to acquire a set of strategies and arm yourself with the necessary tools to effectively navigate interactions with such individuals.

Initially, it is essential to maintain a firm stance, irrespective of the individuals one is interacting with. By displaying firm boundaries, yet maintaining an absence of hostility towards the narcissist, one can effectively maintain relatively amicable relationships while avoiding mistreatment. Under no circumstances should you tolerate any form of bullying, subordination, or unjustifiable and inappropriate demands from others. When encountered with evident indications at the initial stage, it is advisable to promptly dismiss individuals who exhibit narcissistic behavior, provided they are neither your colleague, superior at work, nor a familial relation in proximity. There are ample opportunities available to discover new companions, forge fresh friendships, and engage in pleasurable pursuits. Nevertheless, existence is not always so straightforward, and it is conceivable that you may find yourself contending with a family member or an individual occupying a position of higher authority within a professional context. In such a scenario, how does one effectively manage interpersonal dynamics, preserve positive professional relationships, and safeguard oneself from becoming a victim of narcissistic manipulation?

When engaging with colleagues in a professional setting, it is advisable to ensure that the majority of conversations occur within a communal context. Alternatively, if there is no social pressure exerted, the narcissist might appropriate your ideas or subject you to mistreatment. Narcissistic individuals typically demonstrate an apparent indifference and lack of shame, yet they seek to maintain a carefully crafted persona that attracts a substantial following and garners admiration. This implies that a group environment is not the optimal context for engaging in explicit manifestations of narcissistic abuse. Make an effort to establish clear limitations whenever your supervisor or a coworker attempts to coerce you into assuming additional responsibilities without compensation. Correspondingly, it is advisable to strictly adhere to your own obligations in the event that they attempt to shift responsibility and assign blame to you. It is universally recognized that a highly adverse or morally compromised work setting should necessitate your departure and pursuit of alternative employment. An employer with narcissistic tendencies can present considerable challenges, particularly in cases where they devalue your worth and fail to genuinely appreciate your capabilities. In the event that an individual solely attempts to test the limits of your tolerance and exploit your vulnerability, it is imperative to maintain firmness and demonstrate your unwavering conviction in your desires and boundaries. Additionally, tactfully indicate what you are unable to tolerate. If you observe that an individual demonstrates a resolute intention to subject you to mistreatment through various means, while simultaneously holding social and occupational authority over you, it may be prudent to contemplate seeking alternative employment opportunities rather than devoting energy to developing coping mechanisms for managing the narcissistic individual.

In any alternative scenarios where it is imperative to uphold the integrity of your personal boundaries and authority, it would be prudent to contemplate achieving a position of advantage and inducing the narcissist to rely upon your support. As an example, this could potentially be feasible with a colleague or a family member. Demonstrate that you possess invaluable knowledge or expertise that the narcissist requires. Convey implicit assurances that you possess the capacity to impart mastery of the skill to them. Show no weakness, avoid expressing emotion in front of them, and do your best to appear invulnerable, but also friendly. Refrain from disclosing any personal details regarding yourself or your associations with the narcissistic individual. Upon observing the initial indications of NPD, it is advisable to promptly classify the individual under the appropriate (medical) classification and exercise utmost prudence when interacting with them. It is important to be mindful that narcissistic individuals possess the ability to exhibit charm and ingenuity with the intent of provoking distress. It is imperative to bear in mind the importance of identifying indicators of narcissistic traits to avoid compounding any potential difficulties. Your primary objective should be to ensure immunity against the narcissist's self-centered demands and influences, while maintaining a neutral relationship.

Likewise, when interacting with a family member, one has the opportunity to demonstrate resilience, discipline, and qualities that are deemed appealing to them. As an illustration, you may choose to occasionally offer compliments or present them with a thoughtful gift, in order to appease the self-absorbed family member. This would consequently foster a state of relative tranquility in their attitudes towards you, or at the very least prevent them from harboring animosity. When engaging in interactions with a family member, it is likely in your best interest to seek paths that minimize the occurrence of conflicts. Never criticize the person, but don't allow them to feed their ego with you, either. The crucial factor is maintaining cleanliness and desirability. By adopting this approach, you can exert a measure of influence over the narcissist rather than being subjected to their manipulation and exploitation. Refrain from addressing their emotional needs and ensure that the relationship does not evolve into something different. As an example, in the event that your sister-in-law, who exhibits narcissistic tendencies, attempts to establish a social relationship and expresses a desire to visit you unaccompanied, it is advisable to make concerted efforts to prevent such encounters. If you have already noticed indications of NPD, it is important to be aware that she likely has ulterior motives, such as seeking to ensnare you and possibly making you accountable for certain issues and imperfections she possesses. Maintain well-defined boundaries in your relationships. An individual exhibiting narcissistic tendencies, whether within a professional or familial context, should not be granted the chance to undergo transformation or personal growth. Succumbing to their endeavors to establish closer relations is likely to result in subsequent regret.

When you reach a point where you are about to become entangled in the narratives concocted by the narcissist within their own mind, ensure that you possess a readily available means of departure. Remain vigilant and maintain a heightened level of awareness. Verify all their statements with factual evidence and refuse to allow the narcissist to exploit you as a receptacle for their projections. In the event that it becomes necessary (for instance, if you find yourself participating in a Christmas dinner with a relative), you may opt to attentively listen to a few anecdotes in which they showcase their self-interest and politely acknowledge them, thereby upholding harmony. Nevertheless, in the event that you discern signs of aggression and mistreatment directed towards your person, coupled with a sense of burden from their projections, it is imperative to promptly seek a means of escape. Establish limits, uphold a clear sense of self, and swiftly transition to a different subject matter.

For example, it is possible that the individual exhibiting narcissistic tendencies may seek to diminish your self-worth by insinuating that your decision to change employment is a result of your inadequacy. Suppose the occurrences in your life lack clarity: could you elucidate the reasons for your decision to change your employment? The narcissist lacks true understanding of the situation, but due to their arrogance and desire for superiority, they are inclined to insinuate that you lacked competence, received instructions from your boss to depart, and so forth. What should you do? In the first instance, it is advised not to become defensive. Maintain composure and incorporate solid evidence into the discourse (such as demonstrating previous attempts to secure improved employment or obtaining a new diploma for more suitable prospects). Present the information in a neutral manner, devoid of any emotional implications or supplementary details. Under no circumstances should you allow the narcissist to provoke you with their assumptions or insinuations. Subsequently, exhibit fervent enthusiasm as you discuss your recently acquired employment to some extent. Assertively maintain your position and unwavering perspective without succumbing to intimidation. Smile and joke at will. Subsequently, divert the conversation to a subject of less personal nature. It is advisable to ascertain the importance of avoiding narcissistic projection and abuse, and to strive towards the prevention of conflicts. Select one of two commendations for the narcissist's genuine or perceived attributes in order to prevent provoking their ire or causing them to experience a sense of defeat. Please be mindful that responding directly to the narcissist's provocation will only heighten the conflict. A narcissistic individual seeks validation from others, rather than experiencing direct defeat in competitive situations or intellectual exchanges.

When faced with the challenge of interacting with a narcissistic individual in a professional setting, it is essential to refrain from personalizing any matters and instead prioritize the objective of accomplishing tasks and finding practical resolutions to any potential issues that may arise. The individual exhibiting narcissistic traits is prone to employing a charismatic approach in order to coax and elicit vulnerabilities or personal details from you. Employ subtle tactics, displaying cunning and cleverness, while refraining from overtly attempting to surpass or outdo them. Attempt to shift their focus by introducing 'appropriate' subjects of discussion. As an illustration, you may choose to remark about the brand of their attire (e.g. "The coat complements your appearance splendidly! May I inquire where you acquired such an exquisite garment?"). You may initiate a conversation about a film or a local event (such as, 'Have you had the opportunity to visit that upscale club?') You most likely possess ... given your typical traits and tendencies. In an alternative approach, introduce a related professional topic that is unlikely to elicit feelings of envy. For instance, you could mention a newly found book that could be beneficial for our joint project. If you are interested, I would be happy to lend it to you. Please let me know. There exist numerous approaches to diverting the attention of the narcissist away from your personal life or identity. Maintain a tactful and business-like manner of communication, all the while comforting the narcissist about your sincere intentions, particularly your lack of interest in engaging in competition or posing a threat to their position. It goes without saying that excessive self-referential discussions regarding one's accomplishments are likely to provoke their displeasure. Hence, it might be advisable to meticulously conceal certain aspects of your life from the narcissist, unless they pertain to essential topics that require discussion, such as your doctoral degree or professional advancement.

Finally, it is imperative to emphasize the importance of attentive listening and striving to provide valuable contributions. Do refrain from becoming entangled in psychological manipulations or engaging in endeavors driven by self-importance, unless one possesses narcissistic tendencies beyond their control. Attempt to portray the narcissist in a manner that emphasizes their inherent humanity, without inadvertently glorifying or romanticizing their qualities in any manner. What does this mean? It would be advisable to display a compassionate and accepting attitude towards individuals with the disorder, should you find yourself in a situation necessitating interaction with them. It should be kept in mind that narcissists frequently harbor profound emotional wounds and a sense of insecurity that have contributed to the development of their disorder. Employ your personal powers of persuasion to engage in negotiations with the individual exhibiting narcissistic tendencies, employing a tact that implies the potential for reciprocal advantages. In an endeavor to refrain from engaging in manipulative behavior, endeavor to explicitly demonstrate to them the advantages of maintaining harmony with you and refraining from any attempts to misuse or take advantage of your presence. The crux lies in remaining unresponsive to their manipulative maneuvers, upholding one's autonomy, and reassuring them of one's benign intentions without attempting to outdo or undermine them. There is no need for exerting efforts to accommodate their desires, as doing so may lead them to perceive you as vulnerable. Nonetheless, it is advisable to allow them to maintain the belief that they maintain authority, as long as it does not jeopardize your position or subject you to any form of mistreatment.

One may nod attentively and lend a listening ear as individuals share their accomplishments on a couple of occasions, ensuring it does not develop into a detrimental habit or a recurrent theme in the relationship.

Moreover, one can enhance their observational prowess to gain profound insights into the psyche of the narcissist, all the while maintaining an air of discretion. Gain insight into their motivations (to be prepared if necessary), while maintaining an air of invulnerability and detachment. Narcissistic individuals are inclined to perceive individuals within the framework of black and white, engaging in objectification of others. Should you allow yourself to be constrained, they will swiftly assign you to a predetermined category and employ all of their tactics against you. They undeniably possess ample expertise and proficiency! Therefore, adopt an impervious and inscrutable demeanor while upholding an ambiance of geniality and security.

CONCLUSION

Attaining contentment lies within your sphere of influence. Your life isn't finished. Taking back control initiates with oneself.

Everyone requires aid at certain points in their lives. You need not endure this in isolation.

If you happen to find yourself in a toxic relationship, assistance can be sought from individuals. Seeking assistance from your acquaintances, relatives, a professional advisor, or even a member of the clergy can greatly contribute to your financial recovery.

I serve as indisputable evidence of one's ability to navigate this particular path. You have the capacity to overcome the prevailing circumstances.

No individual should ever experience a sense of confinement within any form of relationship in which their mental tranquility, personal as well as physical well-being, or overall safety is in any way jeopardized or has the potential to be compromised.

You possess exceptional qualities that make you truly remarkable, with a wealth of valuable attributes that you have to offer. It is highly deserving, both for yourself and your children, if applicable, to encounter a special individual who wholeheartedly appreciates and loves you for who you genuinely are, rather than their perception of who you should be.

Imagine, with utmost clarity, the possibility of rediscovering profound joy and relishing once more in the activities that previously brought you immense pleasure. No longer will there be any apprehension regarding what lies ahead. You have finally found contentment in the current situation.

The burden has been alleviated from your thoughts. The shedding of tears ceases indefinitely.

You finally recognize that you are deserving of something better. Although it may seem implausible at present, it is undeniably within the realm of possibility.

If you choose to proceed with this decision today, you will be one step closer to achieving a happier future.

You have the power to bring about this outcome. I have full faith and trust in your abilities. Now is the opportune moment for you to have faith in your own abilities.

Please issue a declaration stating that today marks the commencement of the rectification process. Henceforth, you shall embark on a journey towards fulfilling the remarkable existence that befits you.

Zero Contact

In order to put an end to the emotional roller coaster, two tasks will need to be accomplished.

One of the sole methods by which individuals can successfully navigate the aftermath of a narcissistic abusive relationship and disengage from the narcissistic individual is to implement a complete cessation of all forms of communication with them. You can only commence the process of healing from the pain and suffering you have endured once you have not just closed the door, but also secured it with a bolt and lock, and completely disengaged from any association with those individuals.

The initial few weeks and months of your healing journey will prove to be the most challenging period. Nevertheless, as time progresses, the obstacles encountered and the fluctuating nature of your emotional states will gradually diminish to the point where they are nearly eradicated.

Over the course of time, there will inevitably arise occasional instances where you will encounter something that evokes a past emotion. However, as the years pass, these occurrences will become increasingly infrequent and more widely spaced. (A Conscious Rethink, 2019).

The Process of Reinventing oneself and Revitalizing one's Life

The narcissist in your previous experiences has undermined your self-perception. Now, you are confronted with the task of reconstruction as you move beyond the past.

The process of reconstruction, along with the process of recuperation, requires a considerable duration. It elucidates the necessity for you to confront your fears, inner struggles, and anxiety. It is imperative for you to confront those inner struggles and thoroughly rid yourself of them. These are the vestiges of the individual demonstrating narcissistic tendencies.

These represent injuries and traumas as profound and distressing as if inflicted by a sharp-edged implement. It is now imperative for you to meticulously stitch the wounds and facilitate the healing process of the scars. All these notions pertain to the misconceptions concerning oneself, namely, the notion of being devoid of worth, lacking any inherent value, and being led astray by these fallacies. The erroneous convictions that have arisen from your personal encounters. Before you can construct your new identity, it is imperative that these fallacies are dispelled.

The process of self-reconstruction and restoring one's life is undeniably arduous and fraught with obstacles. On certain occasions, there will be days where you will experience a sense of progress and a positive disposition towards oneself and the pursuit of a new life. However, there will be occasions when you'll experience a sense of stagnation, where it may seem that you're not advancing in any way.

You'll have moments of exultation and confidence then quickly see it turn to misery and hopelessness. This process of reconnecting with oneself bears resemblance to a roller coaster journey; however, by steadfastly persevering, one will eventually navigate through the obstacles, witnessing a decline in adversity while the moments of elation and self-assuredness become more frequent than those of desolation.

(A Conscious Rethink, 2019).

Recovering from narcissistic abuse poses a considerable challenge due to the peculiar tendency of victims to fixate solely on the positive moments of the relationship, convincing themselves that altering their actions could have salvaged the partnership. They envision their former partner bestowing affection upon another individual, fulfilling the intimate yearning they desire.

Such thoughts are customary during the initial stages of the healing procedure. Nevertheless, excessively fixating on this previous abusive relationship for an excessive duration is detrimental to one's well-being and requires addressing.

The process of healing, as previously mentioned, entails experiencing a wide range of emotions. Make every effort to enlist the assistance of a therapist who will provide guidance as you navigate the intricacies of your emotions.

It requires multiple encounters with the harsh truth in order to counterbalance the illusion that was shattered, and embrace the current reality which is truly remarkable and irreplaceable.

Developing Self-Confidence Once More

You are consciously cognizant of the fact that the experience of enduring mistreatment has the potential to utterly devastate and fragment one's sense of self. This can lead to difficulties in placing trust in individuals in your vicinity and can detrimentally impact your self-assurance.

There is a possibility of misjudging individuals or potential acquaintances as Narcissists when they approach you or seek to establish a connection with you. If one fails to exercise caution, they may find themselves leading a solitary existence devoid of the pleasures of companionship and happiness.

However, it is an undeniable fact that such circumstances can be subject to alteration. As you continue to peruse the following text, you will discern the means and strategies at your disposal for assisting in the amelioration of the aforementioned situation.

Following the experience of abuse perpetrated by the Narcissist, you may encounter challenges in effectively rendering decisions, even in matters of minor consequence. "And subsequently, reaching a decision may present a formidable challenge." And it may appear to you that your desires remain considerably distant. You persistently harbor doubts, and these uncertainties are more intimately intertwined with your being than you may realize.

Might the recollection of past events provide assistance? How did it start?

Whilst perusing this literary work, you may have discerned that the issue originated from the manipulative technique of gaslighting. A person exhibiting narcissistic traits has rendered you vulnerable. You will have an observation, however, your Narcissistic partner asserts otherwise, rendering all your defensive strategies ineffectual and futile.

For instance, when observing a television screen, if you happen to notice an item and perceive its color as blue, you might experience astonishment upon realizing that the object in question is actually green. The individual beside you, asserting to possess superior vision, confidently affirms its greenness and firmly maintains this stance. He will proceed by asserting that you have misconstrued the message or possessed an inaccurate perception. As he progresses, one's confidence in their own knowledge becomes subject to scrutiny; their instincts are called into question, resulting in a gradual erosion of strength and an unfortunate adaptation to such ill-treatment.

However, it must be stated frankly that individuals who engage in emotional abuse do not typically do so with deliberate intent. Is that surprising? They have become deeply entrenched in the belief that they are averse to witnessing your ascendancy or your assertion of happiness and welfare.

Their method for enforcing this stance is through the cultivation of perplexity and uncertainty within you.

Consider enduring this phase not merely for one or two years, but potentially persevering for a span exceeding a decade or even two. Having neglected self-care and lacking self-confidence for an extended period of time, you may have developed the mindset that such circumstances are typical for an individual. At a certain juncture, one ceases to inquire.

At that juncture, your well-being and assertiveness have both dissipated. It has been acknowledged by you that you lack warmth, empathy, and affection due to expressing anger in response to mistreatment inflicted by a Narcissist.

Your justifications for experiencing discontent are valid and morally sound. You have encountered a boundary that has been breached. You are cognizant of the fact that despite professing their love for you, they will still exploit and deplete your resources to their own advantage.

All you seem to possess is the assertion that the responsibility lies with you, while your financial equilibrium remains beyond measurable range. This situation engenders a sense of partial trust and prompts a contemplation of one's correctness.

And, as a result, what has the aforementioned circumstances ultimately engendered? Disregard! Self-reliance is not advisable. The lack of trust stems from the abuse rather than from any inherent inability on your part to establish trust. The responsibility for what occurred does not lie with you, but rather with the Narcissists. However, the fact remains that the responsibility for your lack of progress ultimately lies with you. Additionally, rebuilding your confidence in yourself and others is a delicate and considerate process that must be approached with care and sensitivity.

www.ingramcontent.com/pod-product-compliance
Lightning Source LLC
Chambersburg PA
CBHW050026130526
44590CB00042B/1971